Indiana Girls

Night Float

Indiana Girls

Night Float

By: Tara Cleary

ISBN 979-8-9860016-0-9 (Paperback Edition)
ISBN 979-8-9860016-1-6 (e-book)

First paperback edition printed 2022

Cover art by Tara Cleary

In memory of my aunt, Diana Lynn Cleary Fisbeck.

The most beautiful person who ever lived.

She always encouraged me to share all of my talents
with the world.

Preface

I love writing stories and have so many to tell. This is the first one I decided to publish. It's a fun adventure and has a happy ending. This story is pre-pandemic, in a time before we knew the whole world would soon be changed with sadness. I wanted to share this story, because it feels nice to escape into an adventure with friends, outside, in nature. So much of the last couple of years, we have been like prisoners in our own homes. Living lives of solitude, unable to visit with friends or family, not like before. Everywhere we go, faces are hidden behind masks, protecting our hands with gloves or hand sanitizer and or both. Always keeping a safe distance, between ourselves and all of the other people around us, everywhere.

It was important to me to share everything that happened that day and through the journey that night. I chose to share the whole story, even the secrets, because I am sure there are other people out there like me, like us, that can relate to this story.

My friends and I float down a local river on inner tubes, at night. We had never done this before and as you will soon find out, we were very unprepared for this journey. It's fun to try new things, but important to be some-what prepared for whatever you are going to do. Preparation takes the spontaneity out of the adventure, but believe me, you will still have all of the experience and reduce the risk of mortality.

Also, I went forward with actually finishing the publishing process, because life suddenly seemed much shorter than I had previously thought it was. I had been taking my time and the time I spend with the people in my life for granted. Life is too short. Don't wait too long to follow through with plans you have for your life or dreams you want to follow. Enjoy every moment and actually be present in those moments, especially with the people you love. I have been guilty of being distracted during what should have been meaningful conversations. Thinking about work or things I will need to do before the end of the day or week ext. Also, I have been guilty of putting things off, like family visits, because of the long drive. Or not calling someone, because they usually talk for an hour and I don't think I have the time for that. Trust me, give them the hour.

I was able to write this story and remember all of the details of the adventure, because I was sober. I was unaware of all of the little things I had been missing in my life, all around me, until I found them in sobriety. It is like landing in Oz, stepping from a black and white existence, into a colorful one, with shoes that sparkle. Now, when a bird sings, it's just for me. All of the blooming flowers are for me. Every painted, sunset sky, is just for me.

I really hope you enjoy this story and can escape into the adventure with us.

Introduction

Our story takes place during the summertime, in Noblesville, Indiana. Everyone here loves summer, probably because the winter seems to last too long. After the holidays, it can be months of cold gray skies and bare trees and bushes. Also, Indiana weather can be unpredictable during the change of season. Warm one day and cold the next, often with an unexpected snow in the spring. And then bam, it's summer and everything is green. The world is awake and alive. Birds are chirping and signing and people come out of their homes for every reason. To work in their yards or to rest on a chair, in the sun or in the shade, it doesn't matter, because its summertime.

Noblesville was a smaller town when I was born, but has grown a lot over the years. From a few stop lights, to a few more and now those intersections are turning into roundabouts. Corn fields are rapidly disappearing under subdivisions. I used to know almost everyone in passing, now since the population has grown so much, I may only see one person that I know at the grocery store.

My friends and I are from Noblesville and have known each other for a long time. Krystal and I have been close friends since we were 13 and 14 years old. We met on Conner Courts. A community basketball court that used to be next to McDonald's on Conner Street. The basketball court is gone now, but I'll never forget that day.

Back then I spent most of my free time playing basketball. In my neighborhood at the time, Noble Manor Apartments, we had a small court with one basketball goal. The kids would gather there after school and wait for someone to show up with a basketball, so we could play. We would play Pig or Horse or if we had enough people, we would play 21, until the kid with the ball had to go home for supper or do homework. I remember being so happy when I got my own basketball, then I could play as soon as I got to the court and for as long as I was out.

All of the kids in the area were happy when Conner Courts was built. There were several full courts, so an actual game could be played, if you had enough people. I would go there often. There was one goal I played on the most, even alone. The goal in the very back row, on the corner. One day, on my walk up, I could see a guy playing on my court, just him and his dog. Our outfits matched, both wearing white t-shirts and blue jeans. I knew I had never seen him before, because he was the most beautiful thing I had ever seen. I chose the court opposite of him and his dog, trying not to look over, but eventually I think my ball bounced over to his court (my court first). We played a few games and that was that. We would meet at the court and play basketball together almost every day.

He lived down the road, in the opposite direction. So, if I got to the court first, I would look for him to walk up to Conner Street and cross it. One day, I saw him and noticed he was walking with a tall blonde! I had never felt this feeling before, a sick feeling in my stomach, jealousy and rage. I wasn't sure what was happening or what I was going to do.

They approached the goal and I remember standing there in shock. She said "Hi, I'm Krystal. I'm his sister." Relief, followed by disbelief. They looked nothing alike. He had dark hair and dark eyes, she had blonde hair and blue eyes. I kept looking at him and her, back and forth for any similarity, but found none. We didn't play ball that day. I made him take us straight to his grandma's house, to prove to me that they were siblings! We awkwardly walked the four blocks together, to ask his grandma if it was true. She laughed and laughed and confirmed for me "Yes, it's true, they are brother and sister." She kept laughing and laughing. I can still hear her laughing. She was a very sweet lady, never met a stranger and always had food for thought. God rest her soul. He and I did not work out, but Krystal and I remained friends, best friends.

A few years later, when we grew up, Krystal moved to her own place on the other side of town. A cozy community where everyone knew everybody. This is where we met Kisha and Katie, Krystal's new neighbors. In the summer, everyone would get together for a birthday party or cookout and bring a dish for a pitch-in. The smell of a charcoal grill and the food roasting on it would fill the air. Kids would run around laughing and playing and the adults would gather in their lawn chairs, sitting on a porch or in a yard.

Over the years my friends and I have had a lot fun together, but this is one of my favorite memories. One summer, on a Friday night, Krystal and I had planned to go out for dinner, but the plans had changed last minute. Instead of going to a restaurant or a back yard BBQ, we decided to try something new, to float down the river at night! Why not? We had never done that before. It wouldn't cost much money, just the price of an inner tube and any snacks we wanted to bring. What's the worst that could happen?

WARNING:

Rivers are unpredictable and can contain hidden dangers. Learn water safety skills, how to assess risk and how to swim. Wear a U.S. Coast Guard approved life jacket at all times. Even good swimmers need to wear one. Always float, boat or swim as part of a group. Check the weather conditions and current water levels before embarking on your trip. The difficulty level of certain sections of the river can change dramatically with the changes in water level. Write up a float plan and leave it with a responsible person. This can provide valuable information in the event of a search. Take some type of communication device, it is important in the event of an emergency.

Indiana Girls

Night Float

Chapter 1

JD

As we walk into a local diner for some breakfast, everyone looks up from their plates to stare at us. We are a sight. We look like drowned rats and surely smell worse. The place was asleep before we walked in. Keeping my eyes on the floor, I follow the group to the back of the diner. Our waitress is the line leader, shoulder length curly brown hair, wearing a smock top adorned with a white, pin on name tag. I can't make out her name, the room is not well lit. I pull out a sturdy wood chair, to sit at the sturdy wood table.

The morning light dimly shines through a large floor to ceiling window to my left, at the head of the table. Giving us just enough light to stare at the menus with a puzzled look, as if we could not read the language. Sitting up, beathing in the smell of eggs, sausage and freshly baked biscuits. I am so hungry I could eat a horse. Unfortunately, I don't have that much money. Our waitress, with her note pad in hand, walks around our table, quietly speaking to each person. I agree to a coffee and ponder what I can afford from the menu, hopefully before she returns.

Even though it was offered and a very nice gesture, I don't like others to pay for my food, especially, people I don't know. Today, I also wanted to help pay for at least half the group, but I am in a bind. I only have so much money with me. If we had gone to the fast-food joint down the street, I wouldn't be trying to do math in my head, while everyone was ordering. I chose a half order of biscuits and gravy, while my friends order the buffet. Brad, my friend's husband, only orders a coffee and our host orders a special meal. I think everyone frequents here but me.

Even though I have walked past this diner hundreds of times and driven by it possibly thousands of

times in my life, I've only been in here once. When I
was a child, my Grandparents visited from Florida.
Usually, there was at least one day during their visit,
Grandpa would let my sister and I ride with him to the
store, to pick up a newspaper. He would buy us candy
and coloring books. Those were always very special
days. On one occasion, after we picked up the paper, he
drove up to this diner and parked the car. He asked us
"Have you guys ever been here before?" We shook our
heads no. "Well, let's go in and see if they have anything
good to eat!" he said in jolly tone. We were excited and
surprised as we walked up to the door. Grandpa was
always a gentleman, holding the door for us and making
us feel special.

We were seated at a booth, in a line of booths on
a wall of windows. He told us we could order anything
on the menu! I don't think I had ever had that choice
before, neither of us had. Usually, we would be given a
choice between this or that, but never just pick out
whatever you want. I don't remember what I ordered,
but I will always remember what my sister wanted. She
may have not been old enough to read yet and the picture

wasn't on the menu. Very shy, speaking in almost a whisper, she gave us clues to what she wanted. "Something crunchy". Our first guesses were French fries or potato chips, but no. Asking her to look at the menu. "Is there a picture of it?" Grandpa asked sweetly. She shakes her head no. "It's yellow." She looks at me, as if I know what she means to say. Grandpa and I guess and guess, but she shakes her head, none of them are right.

Then, a waitress walks by with a salad and she points to it. Sprinkled on top were little squares of yellow croutons! My sister ordered a bowl of croutons and a coke! Grandpa said we could have anything we wanted and that's exactly what she wanted. I'll never forget that.

Today, it's a nice sleepy diner with good food and a quiet atmosphere. As we hear a group of men pray over their Bibles, a couple tables over, we are reminded this is still a small town. I try not to be too loud, hoping to keep the rest of the group to a hush. I pray too, praying that the words that come from our group do not offend, as much as the very sight of us does.

The girls that order the buffet, get up to help themselves. While the rest of us make small talk, giggling about the night before as we wait for our food to arrive. It's hard to keep my eyes open. I'm ashamed of my hair and what my face might look like. I haven't looked in a mirror since yesterday. All my make-up is probably washed off or I may look like a raccoon. Looking down, I hope to hide my face, while fixing up my coffee. A hand full of single serving coffee creamers and packets of sugar, the real stuff not the pink or blue packets. Not sure why, but they just don't taste the same as real sugar. That's also, probably the reason why I have a little extra weight than the rest of my friends. But weight is the last thing on my mind right now, I can't believe we survived the night! I can't believe we went as far as we did! Wow.

Chapter 2

The Secret

My best friend called to invite me to dinner this Friday night, her treat! We used to paint the town red on Friday nights. I think she still does, after dinner, after we say our goodbyes and part ways, but she won't tell me. I think it makes her sad. Feels like we don't have as much fun anymore, not like before I got sober. There is still a part of me that wants to go too, but I just can't. Sober for about 2 years now and I am going to keep adding up my one days at a time, for now. Sobriety is not hurting me and well, I know if I ever drink again, I would want to smoke a cigarette. I quit that too, dang that was hard. Then I would be drinking and smoking and I would probably become a pirate and sail the seven seas looking for buried treasure and even if we never found it, that would be ok, because I would be drunk on rum and smoking tobacco! It was so hard to quit the both of them. Oh, just thinking about the smell of a Marlboro red before lighting it. Smells like a bag of raisins. Putting fire to the end of that sweet stick and inhaling that warm, full flavor of smoke would be like Christmas, no, better than Christmas, for about ten minutes, until it was gone. Then the sadness would return, well, until I could smoke another!

Friday morning is here. I wear my new coral chiffon shirt and try my best to look pretty. I slip on my gold, sparkle, Jelly shoes, yes, Jelly shoes. Jelly shoes, were my favorite shoes as a little girl. I never wanted to take them off, would even want to sleep in them. I was so sad to grow out of them, couldn't find them in my size after about four years old. I went shoe shopping recently and was truly happy to find some in my size, big foot ha, ha, ha! The shoes complete my outfit. Like a sun kissed peach with a little shine. I was excited for dinner after work, but before dinner, I have one stop to make. It's on my way anyway, my little secret. Or maybe my big one?

I park, put on a little lip gloss and toss my hair as I climb out of my Chevy. I walk up the side walk, to the new entrance. Through the double doors into the new lobby. The pine-sol scent from the freshly mopped tile floor fills the air. Light falls gently from the windows to the left, into a new seating area. I walk past a pair of single stall bathrooms to my right and approach a mirrored glass window ahead. I adjust my eyes to see through the mirrored glass, to a shadow of a person behind it. A woman is holding up a number of fingers. The number is for what computer monitor to go to, where I will be sitting for my visit.

I find my number and sit down on a cold metal stool. A woman I had met before, walks in and sits down on a stool to my left. She turns to me and says "I am so proud of you." I smile, feeling my eyebrows raise in a questioning furrow. She says "I was here the last time you were here. You did a good job standing up for yourself. He is in no position to talk to you that way. I am surprised you are back today after all of that." I smile and nod my head in agreement. Without asking, she tells me "I am here to support a guy I met on a dating website. We emailed and text back and forth for a couple months before we met. Then after our first date, he did something stupid and got arrested. I want to give him a chance, but not sure how long I will wait." I smile and nod in agreement "Me too."

She sits up straight, positioning herself to the camera at the top of the monitor, same as the rest of us. Like picture day at school, when the photographer tells you to sit up straight, chin up, fold your hands gently together on your lap, now say cheese. My monitor lights up and I grab the telephone receiver that is hanging on the side. A little clock is counting down from one minute in the center of the monitor. As the clock hits zero, a login screen appears and we all race to enter our login info to start our visits. The longer it takes, the less time we have for our visit.

My password is validated and another screen pops up with him looking back at me. I can already tell the argument is not over. He has a scowl and we both sit in silence most of the visit. Exchanging hellos and how was your days, nothing much different than every other time. He is upset that he is here and I am just waiting for him to say something nice. He asks me "So, why are you all dressed up?" I tell him "I am going to dinner after this visit." He looks at me sideways "With who?" I tell him "A friend." He will not like hearing I am going out with Krystal. They hate each other. He knows that when we are together it's like fire and gasoline, or well, it used to be anyway. There is no telling what kind of adventure we'll have. That's how he and I met.

Back then, I had been working two jobs for a year. Finally, at the end of the year I quit my second job. My first weekend off, I call her up to hang out. We hit the town with half-gallon of tequila. As I drive out of town, into the sunset, she calls a couple people to see where the party is. I have been out of the loop for a long time. She gets a hold of Jennifer, a mutual friend. She was at a garage party, a couple towns away. She told Krystal we should come. We had never been to any parties in that town before, so why not? We were all dressed up and that bottle was waiting to be opened.

Car parked on a side street, we walk down an ally following Jennifer and her boyfriend. Smiling with our party favors in hand, we approach the garage. We don't see anyone standing around outside and don't hear any loud music. As we follow them in, we see a pool table and only two other guys. I think our looks to one another were obvious. We had been tricked! This is not a party, if it is, it's a sad, lonely quiet one. Oh well, might as well get to drinking. We play pool and take shots till the bottle is half gone, till we're half gone too. At this point we want to go dancing. We all go to a bar down the street. Now we get the party started. The night is filled with loud music, strobe lights, dancing and more drinks.

The next day I hear that I chose this guy, by pushing him up against the wall in the tavern and forcefully kissing him! I guess if I were a cave man, I would have hit him over the head and drug him by his hair to the cave! The rest of the night was filled with trouble too. He knows firsthand and that's why he doesn't want her and I to hang out.

But now, I am not his anymore. We broke up a few weeks ago, before he got arrested, again. He will be transported out of state, any day now. Then he will really be alone. I come to see him about once a week. I think that's what I would want him to do for me, if I were in his shoes. We were together for a while. I probably shouldn't be visiting him now, but a part of me still loves him and it's my choice to make. I keep him a secret because my family and friends would not have anything nice to say about it. I don't feel like getting opinions, so I am not telling anyone anything.

As we sit there looking at each other, he keeps asking me with his eyes. Raising his eye brows and then, finally nodding his head, curling his lips in between his teeth making a straight line, like he knows now, after my long silence. I tell him "With Krystal." He said "Yep." He looks down shaking his head and sighing with a deep breath. He knows that he can't stop me and I remind him "We are not together anymore and I will do whatever I want." Like something a kid would say, that just turned 18. I think he is angrier now than he was when I first arrived! We just sit in silence for a few more minutes.

To break the silence, I tell him "Tomorrow we are going to have a cook out and go floating down the river." He fakes a smile and nods his head. My phone rings five minutes before the visit is over and he hears it. I don't answer, but he knows it's her. I tell him to have a nice night and that I will see him next time. We say good bye and the monitor turns black.

The lady I met before, catches up to me in the parking lot and says "I heard you say you're going out to dinner, have a nice time!" We part ways with a smile as I walk back to my car. The sky is warm, about an hour or two till sundown. Krystal knew where I was, in a visit with him. She called early, probably just to piss him off! Ha, ha, ha, I wonder, is she is going to cancel or is she as hungry as I am?

Chapter 3

Dinner?

I get in the car and call her back. She says "I already started drinking. How about a night float down the river?" I ask her "Don't you want to wait till tomorrow?" She says "Do you want to wait till tomorrow?" I agreed "Let's do it, I'm on my way!" I hear the excitement in her voice as we both say at the same time "See ya soon!"

She lives in the garage party town now. When I get there, I park and walk around the corner of the block. Walking on the side walk, under the shade of tall, old trees. Her husband walks off the porch from across the street and meets me on the side walk. He says "She just left." I ask "She does know I am coming, right?" He shrugged his shoulders and said "Yeah, I think they went to see if they could buy another float at the store. I don't know. She is with Kisha and Katie."

Kisha is our friend, she's a couple years older than us and Katie is her daughter, a very young adult. They look like sisters and like you would imagine, little pixies or fairies to be like. Both tiny, petite little women, very happy and always smiling. You will always find them together, where you find one, you are sure to find the other. Krystal and I are more like, tall, striking Amazons, careful not to mess with us.

With a deep sigh, I walk up to the porch to wait on them. I sit down on an oversized, concrete step, breathing in the fresh summer air. A while later, walking from around the side of the porch, three beauties approach, they are all wearing short shorts, and brightly colored loose-fitting tanks over their bikini tops. I wasn't dressed for the occasion. I didn't know this was what we were going to do, but oh well. Lately since I quit drinking, I have been the odd one out anyway. Either way, I wouldn't have been wearing a swimsuit or bikini. I really haven't been swimming in years. The girls with their beach towels and I with my sparkling shoes, walk to my Chevy, smiling, we all jump in.

Loud music, the wind in our hair, sunroof open and all the windows are down, as the sun sets over the country fields on our drive. Singing and dancing in our seats, smiling at each other as we enjoy the ride. They didn't have any luck finding floats. All the stores they went to were sold out. So, we drive to one more store, closer to the river, to see if we can find some floats there. Music still blaring when we park the car, we wait till the song is over and then get out. With our sunglasses on, we all walk in together.

People notice us wherever we go. I see people throughout the store that I have known my whole life. We walk to the back of the store, where the camping and fishing equipment is, to find our floats and we found some! On the same isle I run into a girl we went to school with. Her sister and I used to walk to and from school together in Junior High. We would all hang out after school, almost every day. I miss them. Those sisters are gorgeous too and there was a time, like Kisha and Katie, they were inseparable. You would always see them together.

We each grab a float, holding our boxes, we make our way to the front of the store. Only four registers are open, each one with a long line. We pick our line and wait. It feels like an eternity when you have something exciting to do next. After a long time, a lady in front of us moves slightly to the right of her cart revealing a sign at the end of the conveyer belt that says *"Next register please"*. My head tilts back to stare at the ceiling, rolling my eyes in anger. I point out the sign to my friends. They shake their heads as if to tell me we aren't going anywhere. With one turn Krystal lifts up the small sign and places it over top of the candy bars and smiles at me with her piercing blue eyes. No one sees a thing. My eyebrows lift and my eyes widen and they all giggle and keep the laughter going by making funny gestures, quietly mocking the woman in front of us in line. Every time she turns away, they mock her, like children do when the teacher isn't looking.

The line behind us gets longer and longer and I feel guilty for it. I feel horrible for the lady that is about to ring us up. My conscience bothers me when it is our turn in line. I feel my neck warm and my face turn red. The cashier smiles and rings us up as if she has already forgiven us. Like she knew the whole time what we had done to her. As soon as we walk away, I feel lighter, better and better with every step we take on our way to the car.

Next stop is to fill up our floats. There is a free air pump across from the old Firestone factory. It was demolished and paved over a few years ago. I remember when the factory was still open, filled with people working. I would walk down the sidewalk next to it, listening to the loud noises that escaped the open windows. They stretched along the building from one end to the other. No air conditioning, that was common in all the older factories. They would use large fans and open the windows to keep the air moving, but ventilation was still a struggle for these old buildings. I have heard stories of people overheating at other companies, operating in similar older buildings, that are still in use today.

Now, the neighborhood is dark and the street light over the air pump is dim. We jump out, I lift the back hatch and start opening the boxes. Pulling out the floats and strings of ropes inside. I hand the flat, rubber smelling plastic to Katie and she passes them to Kisha and Krystal to fill up with air. I break down the boxes making them flat, to give us more room for the floats once their blown up. The girls fill up the floats quickly, like large balloons. Now we try to cram them into the back of the car. Two floats fill the back of the car completely and I bring up the option to tie the other two to the top. The girls disagree. Kisha and Katie get in the back seat and we cram the other two floats in, on top of them. The girls disappear behind the floats, but we can hear their tiny voices answer us "We're ok." then Krystal and I close the back doors.

The liquor store closes in ten minutes! We have to drive straight there to pick up a little bottle for Krystal and Kisha. Kisha carefully gets out of the back, keeping the floats in the car. We all watch her go in and see her smile as she talks to the cashier. She walks out with a big grin and carefully gets back in the car, sliding behind the floats in the back seat, as her little arm stretches out to pull the door closed.

I reverse the car cautiously, because I cannot see through the rear-view mirror, those dang floats. Only using my side mirrors, I pull out and drive onto the street.

Last stop is the gas station for some sodas, a few blocks away.

The girls all walk in to get their drinks and I decide to wait in the car until they return. They all come back and Krystal hands me a couple bucks before I go in for my soda. "Oh, I forgot, will you get me a lighter?" she says. I take her money and my keys with me. They snicker at me saying "We weren't going to leave you!" Smiling as I walk in, grab my drink and walk up to the cash register to pick out a lighter. I see a couple she might love, some with flowers, some with ty-dye or pink and purple designs, but instead, I pick one with a cowboy on a horse. She would never pick this one, but she will laugh at it and remember tonight every time she uses it later. I hop back in the car, hand her the lighter and she laughs out loud and says "What! Look guys!" showing the girls in the back the lighter. "Only you Tara, only you!"

Chapter 4

Jump In

With the radio playing and the sweet, warm summer breeze kissing our faces, we drive a few miles out of town, to the drop point in the river. I have to pay close attention after the stop light for the turn or I'll miss it. I see it and turn in to a gravel drive, flipping my head lights off as we pull in, just in case. I am pretty sure we are not supposed to park here. We get out and are surrounded by trees. About fifty feet ahead, is a utility building. Under a dim security light on a tall wood pole, we drag out all the floats and tie them together.

Once we are ready and all the floats are tied together, we put all the things we don't need, back into the car. Keeping what we do need on our person, in our tops, cause everything from the waist down is going to get wet in the river. I tuck away my flip phone and an extra pack of Krystal's cigarettes. They all tuck away their phones, lighters and cigarettes too. I ask "Does everyone have everything you need? I'm going to lock up the car." All the girls check their stuff again and open the doors to look at what they left behind and then I lock up the car. Together we all say "Here we go!" as we start walking down the soft grassy hill. Each of us holding a drink in one hand and the rope to our floats in the other. Following a trail, we walk into the darkness. It gets darker and darker the farther we walk into the woods, moving towards the sound of the river. The one thing we should have brought was a flash light. Too late now, oh well. Our eyes start to adjust to the dark as we get closer to the river.

As we approach the river, we walk to a large, old tree, standing strong at the edge of the water. Tall grasses and weeds line the bank and surround it. We stop by the tree, standing in the dark. We can hear the water rushing, it's louder now. Krystal says "Here goes!" and we throw the floats into the river. They smack the water and gather together, bouncing off each other like gentle bumper cars, as to say they are ready to go, with or without us. We all look at one another to see who will jump in first. I pass my soda to Krystal and I'm the first to jump in. I hop up into a float and grab the tall grassy weeds, pulling myself closer to the bank. I hold on tight, trying not to get carried away by the current. Krystal passes my drink back and with one hand still gripping the grass on the bank, I put it in the drink holder. Then she passes me her drink and she is the next to jump in. Kisha and Katie pass their drinks to us and then they jump in. Their screams fill the air. The shock of the cold water is overwhelming. Everyone quickly hops into a float and we are all laughing by the time we are ready to start our water adventure. Swinging our arms in the water, like paddles, we push off, making our way to the middle of the river, where the current is a little stronger. We should have brought some paddles too!

Once we are in the current, in the center of the river, a fish jumps out of the water, right next to us. Then another jumps out. We look around and see big ripples moving in the water against the moon light and Kisha and Katie stop paddling, taking their hands and feet out of the water. We all do the same and lean back. The beautiful blue night sky is filled with stars. The banks on both sides are twinkling with fire flies. The fish jumping around us and the glow of nature into a sparkling sky, it's as if we are in a dream, a beautiful dream.

Soon Kisha is on her phone, talking to a guy she had met earlier in the day at a gas station, before they met up with me. The girls tell me about how this fine-looking guy walks up to them and says something smooth to Kisha and she says something smooth back and they exchange numbers. She is busy now, taking selfies and telling us "This is me right now!" tilting her head back with a smile. The constant glow from her phone attracts bugs, but she can't look away. Like those bugs, she too is a moth to a flame. Krystal also has her phone out, but to play music, while we all float down the river singing along.

Even though we have the night sky filled with stars and the fire flies on the banks, it is still dark and we cannot see very well at all. We hear something rustle in the trees and then it drops into the river! It's big and makes a huge splash! The girls scream. Kisha saying "Oh my gosh! Oh my gosh! What was that? Oh my gosh! Oh my gosh!" Katie echoing the sounds of her mother "What was that? Oh my!" Now we all take our hands and feet out of the water again. Actively searching around our floats for ripples, because we cannot see into the water at all. The river is like black paint, reflecting small glows of light, but you can't see through it, not even an inch. We are hoping that whatever joined us in the water isn't hungry.

The girls are now sharing stories they heard on the news of gators and crocodiles in rivers and small local lakes. People had them as pets, but for whatever reason had to let them go. Then they grow into these giant man eaters! I too share a story. "I heard of a shark swimming upstream in a river from the ocean, but luckily that was in the Carolinas!" Everyone is shook-up and scared now. It's like we are sharing scary stories around a camp fire, but in the river. I reassure them "We are too far from the ocean. Oh, and by the way, whatever it was, came out of the trees." But that doesn't help at all. We are all alert, actively searching around our floats, with our eyes on the black water, holding our breath.

A few minutes go by and it was back to relaxing and enjoying the night float, under the sea of diamonds. I am the first to see a large bolder about twenty feet in front us and I tell the girls "It's a rock." This way we can paddle around it or push off of it, so we don't pop a hole in one of the floats.

As we get closer, we lift our legs, bracing to kick off of the bolder. The moment we are ready to push our feet against it, it moves! "Ahhhhhhhhhhh" our screams echo into the air, piercing the night and ringing in our ears. It jumps up, onto its legs, towering over us. My heart is pounding out of my chest. We have no choice but to ride into its mouth or jump into the water with it, a live sacrifice to a river monster. Adorned with a large rack of antlers, it gallops out of the river and into the woods. It's only a deer, a large buck.

Of course, we aren't afraid of a deer, but we couldn't tell what it was until we were right on it. It's so dark! We are all breathing very heavy now. Laughing at each other, we are so freaked out! We hadn't even been in the water an hour yet. Kisha and Katie are ready to get out now. I can't blame them. Kisha is trying to get her new guy friend to come and get us, but I don't think he will. It is late at night and we are somewhere on the river. It would be hard to find us unless we met him at bridge that crossed over it.

The group eventually calms to a silence, drifting to a clearing from the trees. In the quiet country side, the night sky is now holding up an old, concrete bridge. It stretches very high out of the water to meet the road. The sound of a car driving over the bridge above, follows it away, down the old country road. As we approach the massive bridge, I stare up at it and for a moment. I hope for any reason, it doesn't want to fall. As we get closer, Kisha and Katie lift up their feet and push off of a pillar to bounce our floats back into the current. Our voices echo under the bridge, as a reminder of our childhood. Yelling over the water, under a bridge for the first time. The loud, hollow sounds that wish to be repeated.

The current picks up and pulls us back into the shelter of the trees, into the arms of the dark. Crickets and tree frogs send their calls over the banks. The deep hissing rattle of the cicada sounds like bacon frying in a cast iron skillet. We lean back and enjoy the ride.

Chapter 5

Night Fishing

Kisha is now smiling from ear to ear, gazing into her glowing phone. As she swats the bugs away, she tells us "This is me right now!" Her daughter Katie smiles at her, then smiles at us and leans back to smile at the sky. Krystal reminds us "This was a great idea! I'm having a great time!" We all agree with her.

Krystal and Kisha pass a drink between them. Stealing a quick drink and hiding it away again. As if they want to keep it a secret from me. They are my friends and they know I've been trying so hard to be good. If I change my mind about being sober and choose to fall off the wagon and start drinking tonight, that little bottle would be gone in one second! One drink is too many and a hundred, is never enough, not for me. This is my reminder to stay sober tonight. That little bottle would be a start, but there aren't any bars serving drinks on the river banks. Besides, I don't have enough money with me to satisfy my thirst, even if there was such a bar.

The branches jostle in a tree to our right and something falls in! Splat! Panic rushes through us, but before we are able to scream, a second tree shakes on the other side of the river and splash! We pull our hands from the water and put our feet up on the floats or up on the ropes connecting us. What could that be? I don't think a raccoon would do a high dive and then land on a belly flop into the water. I don't think beavers climb trees. Possums hang from trees and are half blind, so maybe they are possums? Huge river rats? I have no idea. Just hoping they're not river monsters.

A few quiet minutes go by and we start to relax again. We are now floating up to Potter's Bridge. It's an old wooden, covered bridge painted white. I believe it may be the last one left in town. Tonight, it's lit up with soft, glowing lights in mason jars, strung across the outside of the bridge. So romantic. Between the bridge, the stars and the fireflies, it truly is like a dream. This is one of the most beautiful nights of my whole life. I can't remember a prettier one. We float up to the soft glow of the covered bridge, slowly glide under it and slip further away. The light from the glowing bridge, slowly dims behind us. The blanket of darkness welcomes us back in again.

Another bridge is up ahead. The street lamps light up the bridge and the river below. We are getting closer to town. The radio is playing some good music and the current starts to slow down. We come to a shallow part of the river, just under the bridge, then we get even slower. The grassy plants push up through the water, waving to us as we drift by. We see some shadows ahead, figures standing in the water. This time we can see, it was a group of fishermen. One of them spots us and signals for the others. They part to make way for us to move through them. One cheeky guy is smiling like he just hit the jack pot, telling us "That looks so relaxing. Have fun girls!" We smile and giggle. Krystal saying "If I wasn't married."

And I was thinking well I'm not! Ha, ha, ha! Kisha is all smiles, but drawn back to her glowing phone.

Good music is still playing and most of us are enjoying the night. Kisha has decided to call her knight in shining armor to rescue her. As they talk, Krystal and I maneuver us around some fallen trees in the river. These trees are stretching their hands up, out of the water. They are reaching for another hand to pull them from the river. I feel sorry for them, knowing they were once part of the family of trees on the bank. Wondering if it was lighting or just a strong wind that tore them from their roots and pushed them into their watery graves.

I keep paddling, but we are headed straight to another log. Krystal pushes off of it with her feet. We are a giant ping pong ball in this part of the river. Our group of floats spins off of one log and towards another. Katie and I brace for it. Our feet out, we push off it, bouncing back into the current. With a deep breath, we paddle hard with our arms, trying to keep in the center of the river. If we pop a float, we could be in trouble.

We see ripples in the water ahead, its rocks. "Butts up!" Krystal shouts, as we all lift our bodies, trying to make our weight even over the donut balloons we are floating on. Wincing and hoping not to snag a jagged piece of rock. We are moving faster here, the river is pushing us, pulling us and then, we hit deeper water around the bank and slow way down.

Kisha is now talking to her guy again and the conversation slowly turns into an argument. It turns out, that he was never on his way to come pick us up. He had been lying the whole time. She is so mad. She accidentally drops her pack of cigarettes into the water. She quickly saves them, but in her rage, she tosses them behind her, back into the river! She tells us "This is me right now and I am in my feelings!" We all laugh with her and can't believe she just did that. It's not like she can buy another pack at the next bridge. Ha, ha, ha. Then, Krystal and Kisha pass the bottle and hide it again.

We float down the river a little longer and come up to a local bait and tackle shop. We surprise two guys fishing off the dock sitting on their coolers. I can tell they are happy to see us. One yells over "What's a group of girls doing floating down the river in the middle of the night?" We answer back "Having fun!" They laugh and remind us "Be careful out there tonight!" We assure them "We will!" and we keep floating by, toward downtown, heading to the twin bridges.

The group is starting to get sleepy. Krystal's phone dies and the music stops playing. In the few minutes it takes to get to the twin bridges, I look over and Kisha is fast asleep. The bottle is gone, her smokes are gone and I guess her phone died too. Might as well take a nap! We are now drifting close by to Krystal's mom's house. She lives less than half a block from the bank. This is the last point before we drift into the unknown. There is a lot of river between here and where we think the next bridge could be. Krystal looks at me and says "Are you ready to get out? I'm not. I'm having a great time!" I agree with her and so does Katie, with a big smile. We agree to let Kisha sleep a little longer. What could it hurt?

Chapter 6

Waterfall

We float past a strip of land, a little island in the middle of the river. One time, when I was younger, I imagined running away to live on that little island, maybe for a summer. Something like Huck Finn or Mud. It was big enough to pitch a few tents on and have a bon fire for a party of five or six people. A secret oasis in the middle of town. We pass the South Side Cemetery on the left and a few houses on our right. We can't actually see the houses, but can see the lights are on, through the trees of the forest. I can't recall if I ever knew about them, trying to think of what street they are on. I had walked almost every inch of this town. I thought I knew it like the back of my hand. The night seems to get darker and the river feels deeper and we are moving faster now. Kisha is fast asleep and we're all quiet. My own eyes are heavy and I think about taking a nap too. Maybe I will, maybe I shouldn't.

An uneasy feeling turns my stomach when I hear the sound of a waterfall. Oh shit! I can't remember driving or walking this far down the river. I don't know if there is a dam. None of us have ever been this far down the river, other than driving over it on bridges. The next bridge I can think of is a few miles down. The sound is getting louder and louder and I begin to panic. I am awake. "Wake up Kisha!" I call to her "Wake up!" I shake her float, but she doesn't move. We all yell at her "Wake up!" I start to paddle us closer to the bank. Krystal pulls the rope and drags us back into the current. Shaking my head, I tell her "There is no way to know if the drop is a few inches or a few feet!" "Sounds like fun! Let's find out!" she says. I keep trying to wake up Kisha, but she is dead to the world. I tell the girls "We need to give her a fighting chance! If we come up to a big drop, she needs to be awake! She needs to make the choice herself, back to shore or be ok with falling into a mystery. Could be a big pile of rocks, fallen trees or it could be a dam!"

The sound gets closer and closer. I can't see a drop ahead yet, but it's so dark and I try to keep my focus on the river in front of us. Keeping track of the distance between us and the tree line on the bank. We come up to a large cement pillar. It looks like it used to be a part of a bridge or maybe an old a mill. A couple hundred feet down on the opposite side, there is another pillar. If this was a bridge, it did not go straight across the river, but at an angle. I don't think it was a bridge. There is no road, no buildings.

The falling water is now very loud. I am alert and ready to jump off my float if I have to, but I don't see a drop. It was either fast water hitting the rocks here or maybe there is a water plant close by on another finger of the river. We are now drifting away from the sound and I am in shock! I cannot believe that's all it was. We are so lucky! I am feeling better, but the uneasy feeling is still in my stomach as we float through the woods alone.

Floating around a bank, we can see a camp fire in the distance. Krystal and Katie are excited, but they haven't seen as many scary movies as I have. I don't say a word. I have already flipped out over nothing and I feel silly about it. Their excitement rises as the temperature in the water seems to drop. We have been in the water for maybe three or four hours now and we are freezing. The sun has been gone for a long time and the water seems to be rising or the river is getting wider.

I don't know who might meet up here and my instincts say we should keep floating on by. Better to be safe than sorry. I would rather stay in this freezing water and float to the next bridge, than take a chance with some strangers in the back woods. It is surprising how unpredictable people can be. When given the opportunity, some people turn into monsters, doing evil things when no one is watching or when no one is there to stop them.

Better to float on by, than to take a chance on finding some crazy guys with a gun. Could be anyone. Could be a family camping? No, not this late at night. Must be around one or two o'clock in the morning. Maybe it's a group of friends? Maybe it is a pair of couples on a weekend camping trip, hoping not to be found? Could be an escaped convict or maybe a future one.

Chapter 7

Camp Fire

We float quietly in the cold dark, that keeps getting colder and darker, except for that little ember of fire in the distance. We expect to approach the fire anytime, floating for a long half hour or so, before coming up to the fire. It is amazing how our eyes can see light from so far away, in the dark.

Drifting faster now, we approach a small beach just off of the edge of the woods. Of course, the first thing to catch my eye are the figures next to the bright light. Two men standing in their underwear! I blink my eyes for the first time in a while and they widen in surprise. I hold back my laughter because I don't want to be rude. We may have interrupted a Brokeback Mountain story. Why else would these guys be standing in their underwear? They must have thought they were all alone and that no one would ever find them. It was a perfect place to make a secret camp for a night, well, it was.

One guy looks over at the other with a smile and waves to us. He says "Hi". Krystal and Katie say "Hi" back. We are floating by quickly and I hope that we say goodbye just as fast. One of the guys says something and we can't make it out. He yells out to us again, but we still can't understand. I shrug my shoulders, shaking my head to my friends. Krystal looks at me and I shake my head again. It is a silent vote, but once she looks at Katie it's two against one.

Krystal jumps off of her float and at the same time loses one of her flip flops. It floats over her shoulder, past her head and keeps floating down the river. The water is deep here, way deeper than we thought it would be. She demands to me "Give me your shoes!" I tell her "No!" She looks at me with distain and demands again "Give me your shoes!" and I say "No, you'll lose them in the mud under the river!" She turns her head to ignore me. Fueled by her anger, she starts pulling us to shore. I didn't want her to lose my shoes too. Walking against the current, through muddy sand, can suck your shoes right off your feet. Besides, I don't want to go to the camp fire. Her strong drive pulls us close enough to the bank, that I jump out and help pull the floats the rest of the way to shore. Katie is on her feet now too and Kisha, well, she is still asleep! Krystal and I grab the handles of Sleeping Beauty's float on either side and pull her up out of the water and onto dry land. Amazons, Vikings, well, you get the picture.

We stand there in the dark, about one hundred feet from the fire. One of the men calls to us, inviting us over to get warm. I am still very leery of the whole thing. I look down at Kisha and back at them and shake my head. I watch Krystal and Katie walk away, shivering with their arms crossed, they quickly walk to the fire. I was warmer in that cold river, now I am freezing.

I keep my eyes on my friends as they stretch their arms out over the glowing, warm light. The men move some things from by the fire to the tent. One walks back to the fire and the other walks away from the fire and into the woods. This grabs my full attention. My eyebrows lift and I look around us. My ears perk up to hear the sound of breaking twigs and branches in the dark woods behind us. We really don't know how many people are here. We also don't know if there is a house or a road nearby. If we needed to run, where would we run to? If we had to jump back into the river, onto our floats, our getaway would be too slow. One of us would get caught and since all our floats are tied together, we would have to either cut the rope, if we had brought a knife or jump out to survive. Well, I can't really imagine that I would cut any of my friends loose to save myself and or the rest of the group, but my brain needs to think of every possibility to make a plan. The water is too deep here and I know I can swim, but I'm not sure about my friends. What kind of friend am I? At this point I realize, we should have brought a flashlight, a paddle, a knife, or machete and some life jackets, ok that's better. Or, like I wanted to do, just kept floating down the river.

Dragging a large, heavy branch, the size of a small tree, a half-naked man walks out of the woods, from the same place he went into earlier. He tosses it into the fire and the embers sprinkle into the air. Glowing dead leaves meet their watery death in the dark river. A few minutes go by and the glow of the fire is burning into my eyes again. As if I am a moth to the largest, brightest flame I have ever seen. I am freezing, burrrrrrrr. I know I was warmer in the water.

Now, I am standing here in the cold dark, wondering if my friends are going to be murdered if I look away. Scary things like that happen quick. The element of surprise is a tactic for murderers and serial killers. My thoughts run wild while I stand here alone. Heaven forbid, what if my sleeping friend isn't asleep? She didn't wake up when we were yelling at her and shaking her float. She hasn't made a sound or moved in a long time. She was like dead weight when we pulled her float up, out of the water and placed her on the beach. I look away from the fire and I stare at her to see if she is breathing. My eyes widen to adjust to the dark. Her shoulders move as she breathes in and I take a deep breath with her. I am glad she is still alive and hopefully we all stay that way.

Krystal walks back to me and says "Come on, come over here with us to the fire." I am standoffish. Katie comes over too, urging me to go over to the fire to get warm. Reluctantly, I agree, following as they lead the way. I feel bad leaving my friend in the float, sleeping by the river. I can feel the heat as we get closer to the fire, the warm light touches my face. One guy to my right and the other off by the tent to the left. I am pretty sure now, after all this time, the men are alone. Only two for me to keep an eye on, while also looking back to Kisha.

One guy starts to speak to us "We were asleep in the tent and the water woke us up! We had to jump out of the tent and move it back, closer to the trees. All our gear is wet, even our clothes are soaked. That's why we are in our tighty-whities!" I could see now, they had draped their clothes over some dead branches by the fire, trying to dry them. He said "The river is rising quickly. It must have rained north of here." As I look down to the bank, a few feet from the fire, I focus on the edge of the water. I do notice that the water is rising. The water is getting closer and closer to us, as we stand right here by the fire.

Krystal and Katie want to bring the floats over to the fire to sit on. Once again, I don't agree. I am on the edge of being a party pooper. Being sober, I feel like I am the odd one out. Could I be the voice of reason or the Devil's advocate? I think this could be a bad idea. It's a rocky beach, if one popped a hole, then what would we do? Would Katie and her mom be able to stay above water together on one float? But as I quietly protest, they walk over and untie their floats. I walk over to them and express my opinion "I would rather mine stay by the water, away from the fire." One of the guys walks over and offers help "You need help carrying your friend over to the fire?" and like a gentleman, he grabs one handle and Krystal and I grab the other, bringing her float about one hundred feet, all the way over to the fire. There is no time to untie my float that was still tied to hers. All the while, my float drags on the ground behind us. Ahhhh! I shake my head in anger, hoping it doesn't snag any rocks or sticks on the sand. We plop her down and she is still sleeping, dead to the world.

I stand behind the three girls as they warm up in the light. Krystal asks me "Let me see the phone." I pass it to her. I am ready to leave as soon as possible. She tries to call her husband, but no answer. She tries over and over and still no answer.

The guy that helped us carry Kisha over to the fire, we will call him Half-Naked Guy. Every few minutes he pulls the branch with his clothes draped over, closer to the fire. After about three times, he accidently flips them over and they land too close to the fire. He picks them up and hangs them back on the branch. I notice glowing embers on his pants, "They are on fire!" I say, and he grabs them and dunks them into the water again. We are all laughing. Now there must be a giant hole in them and they are all wet again, poor Half-Naked Guy. He will have to stay half naked for a while longer. But nice eye candy though!

The guys both walk over to a cooler to our right to grab a couple beers. Krystal says "Can I get one of those?" but I don't think they hear her. They are preoccupied, quietly talking to themselves. She looks up at me. I am already standing up and just a few feet away, so I walk over to them and ask for a couple beers. They say "Sure! What kind?" They had a variety of it. This was odd to me, because when you travel in the wilderness you try to pack light. Not sure if they had brought the leftovers from their fridge, from parties before or had expected others to join their party tonight. Usually there is only one or two choices of drink. I shrug my shoulders and look back to her, as they raddle off more than five or six choices. She picks her poison. Double fisted I walk back to the fire and hand her both. Since I am not drinking, she might as well have her fill. This is her reward to enjoy. It was her idea for the night float, her will power to jump off her float and her strength to pull us all to shore, to the warmth of the camp fire.

As we stare into the fire, the guys start walking around us, packing up their things. They are arguing under their breath about leaving. They walk over to the tent and stand in front of it, arguing, shaking their heads and moving their hands. Then they both go into the tent and walk back out together. Each holding a handle, on either side of a large duffle bag. You can tell it's very heavy. Their arms droop down, and they struggle to keep it from dragging on the ground as they quickly walk to one of the kayaks and drop it in. They both walk back to the tent and grab more things and carry them to the kayaks.

My imagination runs off with me as I think about what could be in that bag. Was it a body? Was it full of money? It was too heavy for money, unless it was half cash and half gold bars, so I go back to the body scenario. Maybe that's why they were arguing. They didn't plan on us floating by, let alone stopping to join them. Maybe they were going to bury it in the woods or drop it into the rising river?

It is clear now that one of them has to be somewhere early in the morning. Or that's the story and he is sticking to it! Half-Naked Guy wants to stay and enjoy the night. Who could blame him? Four beauties floating by in the middle of the night. Like mermaids that magically grew legs, we walked out of the water and onto their beach. We are here now, on this summer night, sitting by their fire on the little beach by the river.

I ask "What time were you going to leave if the water didn't wake you up?" They in unison agree "Around five." I then state "That's a couple of hours away." They explain that they can't find one of the ores. It may have been carried away by the water that woke them up in the tent earlier. They are afraid of running late, now only having one ore. We help them look all over the beach and around the kayaks, but nothing.

Awkwardly, we wander back to the fire as the guys keep packing. A stream of water hits my feet around the same time Katie jumps up and says "My butt's wet!" The river is swallowing the beach. Soon it will be gone, under the water. We should leave too. Krystal borrows my phone and tries to call her husband again, over and over, but still no answer. Kisha is still asleep.

The guys fold up the tent and pack up the kayaks quickly, but Half-Naked Guy drags his feet and still wants to stay longer. The other guy argues that the boats need to stay together. He needs Half-Naked Guy to help pull the weight of all the gear in the third kayak, tied to their two.

I tell Krystal "We should leave too." And she says "Let's wait. Let them get down the river some before we go. I want to build my own fire." I shake my head and tell her "The water is coming in too fast and it will be a waste of time." But once she gets an idea, like me, we are head strong to see it through. We can be very stubborn.

Krystal needs some shoes to walk off the beach and into the woods. Against the whole idea and already refusing my shoes to her before, she borrows Kisha's flip flops. Carefully slipping them off of her feet as she sleeps. I stand there wondering if they would fit as Krystal pushes her feet in, knowing that they will have to do.

Not wasting any time, she walks into the woods at the same place Half-Naked Guy came out with that limb before. She is my best friend, so I follow to help her. It is so dark in the woods. Out of the light of the stars and away from the fire on the beach. I follow closely behind her and pass her my phone. It's a flip phone and glows only when open, for a moment and then it dims again. She finds a large limb and we drag it out together, towards the beach. While our arms and legs are being scratched by the brush of the forest, Half-Naked Guy walks over to help pull the limb out some more. He's being a gentleman. Krystal picks a spot for her new fire over by where we first landed out of the river. Where I stood guard by Kisha as she slept.

Half-Naked Guy walks back into the forest one last time and finds a large piece of wood. Picking it up, he looks it over, end to end. His new ore. This is what a Viking or a Native American would do. Back before there was a sporting goods store in every town. His friend is already in a kayak, waiting for him in the river. Dragging his feet and shaking his head while looking down, he angrily hops in his kayak and plops down. We can hear the defeat in his voice as he speaks, telling us "Goodbye girls!" We say "Thank you for everything and be safe!" His friend is now floating in the current, drifting with the second kayak full of gear and it's tied to the third. Like children holding hands as they walk together and one decides to sit down. Half-Naked Guy reluctantly pushes off the beach with his log. We hear the hollow sound of the kayak as the rocks drag under it. His boat is quickly parallel with his friend's, making a V shape in the water as they pull their gear behind them. One guy paddling with an ore, the other with a large piece of wood. It just might work.

Chapter 8

Wake Up

Sleeping Beauty

Krystal and Katie are huddled around their big branch, trying to get a fire started. It feels as though I am standing in a dream. I am so tired, I just want to crawl into the woods and go to sleep, but I can't. This beach and even part of the woods will all be under water soon. We need to leave now. I feel this uneasy panic inside and all the while, Kisha doesn't have a care in the world. She sleeps with a smile on her face.

The water keeps inching its way onto the beach. Sending little fingers of water over the land before the arm pushes through. I hear a scream, that is followed by a moan. Kisha is awake. An icy finger of water has found its way to her and woke her up out of her warm slumber. The water has circled around the first fire and will soon swallow it. She slowly stands and pulls her float with her, closer to the woods out of the way of the water.

Standing there in shock, staring at us with anger and confusion Kisha tilts her head and exclaims "What is going on?" Krystal and Katie are still working on starting their fire. Looks like a little smoke is stringing up into the air. I don't want them to be successful. If they get that fire started, they won't want to leave until the water carries us all away with it. I explain to Kisha "We came up to a camp. Two guys had a bon fire and we pulled you up out of the water. You would not wake up for nothing. We yelled at you, shook you, but you still wouldn't move. One of the guys took one side of your float with me and Krystal on the other and we carried you over to the fire to keep you warm. It must have rained north of here, because it is starting to flood!" I exclaim, "We must get back into the water to float to the next bridge, so Brad can find us!" Krystal, Kisha and Katie all shake their heads. No one wants to get back into the water, we are freezing, even on this summer's night. I'm sure the water is even colder now and carrying debris.

I explain "Come on guys, the longer we wait, the higher the water will get. It will be better to hurry up and get back into the water now. The quicker we do, the faster we can get out of the water and go home. Or we could walk through the woods until we come to a road. It's so dark and really there is no telling how far we would have to walk or who we might run across. I've seen a lot of scary movies guys."

Reluctantly, everyone gathers their floats. Katie ties her mom's float back in with the group. We wade in the water for a moment, yelling and shrieking at the cold water, trying to jump back on the floats. Our half dry legs making squeaking noises on the wet rubber floats. Krystal is the last one standing, as our floats pull into the river, she keeps us from floating away. She really wants to stay and no one was leaving until she is ready to go. Finally, she hops up on her float, one big splash and we are off.

This time the water is much faster and pulled us out to the middle of the river in seconds.

Quietly floating in the freezing cold water, we are hoping to get closer to a bridge or a road. Searching the world around us for car lights, listening for any sign of morning traffic. No one says a word for a while. Everyone is uncomfortable and cranky. I am racking my brain trying to think of the next road that has a bridge, thinking we should be close, but no. I feel a heavy weight of failure the longer we float.

We turn a bend and the sun begins to break through the horizon. The dark silhouettes of the trees standing in the soft orange sky. The river is light muddy brown. The birds in the trees look down, chirping their gossip about us as we float by. Hopping from tree to tree alerting the next tree of birds as to say "Hey, look there, wild humans are floating down main street!" The banks are full to the brim, pushing against the weeds and tree trunks on the edge of the land. We keep looking for another place to land out of the water, but no luck.

Krystal asks "Let me see your phone again." She calls Brad and he answers! "Hey are you close?" she says to him, then a pause and she says "No we are in the water, somewhere between downtown and 146th street." She listens some more and then she says "Guys, he is in the area and is honking the horn!" We all pause to listen closely, but hear nothing. She says "We don't hear you, drive a little farther and honk again." We all are listening on the edge of our floats, but hear nothing. Over and over, back and forth for about 20 minutes, but still no luck. The battery on the phone is almost done. She looks down at the phone and tells him "I'll call you back when we see a bridge or hear your honking cause the battery is almost dead." She passes me the phone and it drops in the water! I snatch it up, but it is too late. The phone is all wet and the battery is dead. Now we have to find a bridge or a road and hope he happens to find us.

We hear the beeping sounds of something. Could that be him honking? The beeping sounds get louder. We start to float pass another finger of the river and the sounds get louder. But it was not honking, it was the sound of trucks backing up. Excitement runs through me and I say

"I think that's the rock quarry on River Road!" We listen and can hear trucks driving around. My heart beats faster and I feel better about choosing the river over the dark woods. Walking in the dark, we could have fell into the quarry.

Everyone wants out now. Surely if we hear those trucks, we aren't far from the road. All in agreement we search the banks of the river for a place to get out. We spot a place to the right, but the water carries us away before our arms can paddle over to it. Another place comes up on the left, but the same, the water is too fast for us and we pass it by. We stay closer to the left, hoping another place comes up.

A little beach of pebbles shaded by a tree is spotted. Krystal and Katie jump out and pull us up to the tiny shore. We pull the floats up and drop them softly on the rocky beach, trying not to snag a hole. That's the last thing we need, especially if we have to get back into the water, the last thing we want to do.

Kisha and I stand by the tree, trying to dry off in the morning wind. Krystal borrows Kisha's flip flops again and her and Katie venture off into the field of tall grass and weeds looking for a road. Kisha and I wait on the little pebble beach. The bright reflection of the morning sun is blinding. We look down at our feet. I see tiny sea shells, an earring, a piece of a watch, little lost things from the people that came here before us. I keep my eye out for a wallet or bag of gold.

They have been gone a while. Kisha and I walk into the weeds a few feet and our legs get cut up by stinger or sticker weeds. Kisha yells "Ouch!" I agree! We walk back to our little beach and wait. Not sure how much time has gone by, but we are almost dry. Krystal and Katie come back. We are hopeful that they found the road, but no. "Brad is out there looking for us right now." Krystal sighs. "We need to get back into the water and float down some more." No one wants to. We are all so tired and cold. We whine and complain to each other and curse at the water now, but after shaking our heads and shrugging our shoulders, we gather the floats and jump back in.

Chapter 9

Who Can

Swim?

We are drained of energy. I feel like I could sleep for days. This time we are not as loud as we were before, when the water grabs us with its cold hands. We are over the river and want to get out of the woods and don't care whose grandma's house we go to, as long as it is warm and dry, ha, ha, ha!

Krystal grabs my arm and looks down at her feet. She broke a flip flop. One of the straps popped out and she quietly pulls it off, trying to fix it in secret. Propping her shoulder up and turning to one side, she tries to mend the shoe, pushing the strap into the foot of the sandal. Kisha may kill her for this, they were some special, name brand, top of the line, designer flip flops. Worth more than a nice dinner for the four of us at the best restaurant in town. Oh no! At this moment, again, I am glad I kept my shoes and that I mostly shop at Wal-Mart! She tries and tries to fix it, but it won't go back together. She finally looks at me, sighs and flips it over her shoulder, behind her, into the river.

My attention has been on Krystal and the flip flop for so long, when I look up, the river is now four or five times as wide as it was before. It is a muddy light brown, like watching a nature channel when the rains finally come to Africa after a long drought. The water must be very, very deep and I don't know if everyone can swim.

Kisha and Katie are to my right. Kisha is panicking and wants to get out of the water right now. She is arguing with her daughter. She turns over onto her knees, balancing on her float as she stretches her arms over both sides to hold the handles. She slowly stretches one leg down into the water and then the other. Dangling her legs over the edge while balancing her body on the float. She tries to find the bottom of the river, but can't touch the bottom. She keeps her legs in the water with hope to find a rock or something she can touch with her feet, but loses her balance and flips over into the river. Katie screams "Mom! Mom! Mom! She can't swim!" Kisha bobs back up, grabbing her float, gasping for air. Before I can say anything, Katie jumps into the water to help her mom. Krystal and I are paddling our arms backwards with all the strength we have left, trying to keep the floats close to the girls in the water. The current so strong and the water is deep. I want to jump into the water, but one or both of them could pull me down in their panic and I could drown. That's one thing I can remember about first aid and water safety. But it doesn't help, I still feel helpless.

Krystal and I manage to get the floats over to the flooded bank, as quickly as possible. Kisha and Katie are still in the water. Katie tries to push her mom up onto the float, as it flips over. Katie tries again and no luck. The water is trying to pull us away. Krystal and I are gripping to some grassy twigs on the flooded bank and hold on tight. We wait as Kisha and Katie doggy paddle against the current, to try again. This time Katie grabs the float and gets on the other side of it, reaching her arms over to Kisha and they both pull. Finally, Kisha slides up and is back on her float. Katie doggy paddles to her float and climbs up with the last bit of her energy.

She turns over to lay back on her float, breathing deeply and closing her eyes, thinking of how close her mom came to death. We can all breath now. We are very thankful and so very lucky they made it out of the water and back on their floats.

We are overwhelmed by the massive body of water, exchanging our worried looks, scared to go back into the current. There is no place to land out of the water, all the land around the river is flooded and no bridges are in sight. We need to push on, we must be getting closer to the next bridge. Finally, Krystal and I look at each other, we know what we have to do. We let go of the twigs and let the river carry us away.

Another finger of the river flows into our current. We are now in the middle of a large mouth of the river, wider than the length of a football field. It is very deep here and no safe place to swim to. The current has slowed a little, but still moving steady.

It feels as if we were on the ocean. I am secretly hoping not to see a shark fin or the wave of an alligator tail. There would be nothing we could do. Maybe one or two of us could swim to shore, if we went in opposite directions. Hoping there is only one river monster and for it to be the slowest water predator in the world. I think even a turtle would win a race against us in the water right now. At this point, I would bet on a piece of floating drift wood to make it to shore before we do. If we had to escape a shark, let's face it, we would all die. Sitting ducks on a large, muddy ocean of water. We must float together, stay together, our little raft of floats.

Chapter 10

Are We There

Yet?

Panic rushed through us like being on a roller coaster, the sound of the metal clicking as we climb to the top. Panic building as we climb, higher and higher, click, click, click. What are we going to do? The phone doesn't work, we can't call for help. Wishing to see a bridge soon, hoping Brad is still out there, looking for us. I hope he has a rope to pull us to shore.

We are all so tired. If we did decide to paddle to one side or the another, it may be the last thing we do. So, we have to wait until we find a sure landing. If we do find a place to land, nothing is going to get me back into the water. I rather walk through a field of sticker bushes than risk my friends drowning again. I'm so tired, I think I may need to rest and take a nap before the long hike anyway. Like people that wash up on a shore after a ship wreck, resting face first on the beach, before getting up.

Time goes by in silence. I think we float left when we pass a fork in the river. There's no changing course, the current is so strong and we are too tired. Gradually, the river seems to be shrinking. The trees are getting closer to us on both sides, growing taller as the water seems to get shallower. Maybe most of it went down the other side of the fork. We are still holding on, hoping to come to a bridge soon.

No one speaks, everyone's thoughts are also floating away or empty, like our stomachs. It's been hours since we ate and hours since the girls have had a smoke. Kisha might be regretting tossing her smokes over her shoulder last night. Krystal may be dreading having to tell Kisha about her sandals. Katie is probably glad she came, at least she saved her mom from drowning. I regret us not getting out downtown last night, but we would have never found the guys on that little beach with the camp fire. Or felt the excitement of thinking we may meet our fate with a waterfall or possible dam. What were we thinking? None of us had life jackets on, no one knew if the other could swim. We didn't even think of finding out if it had rained north of us before we went. So many things I would do different next time. Wait, who the hell would do this again?

Off in the distance we hear people. Their voices seem to echo, like they are under a bridge! My heart beats faster and faster. We all sit up and look at each other with smiles. We float around a bend and see a bridge. We all start to paddle, trying to get there faster. In the distance, we see a man fishing, wading in the river, the water about knee high. Paddling faster now, we come to some tall grass sticking up out of the water. It's time for me to stand up. One by one we stand and walk closer to the bridge. Kisha makes a frown, her feet hurt walking on the bottom of the river. She asks Krystal "Do you have my sandals?" Krystal saved one and threw it to her and it smacked the top of the water. "Sorry, the other one accidently broke and I lost it in the river." Kisha sighs, and says "I hate this old river!" she doesn't reach down to pick it up from the water, she lets the sandal float away, no need to save it without the other. Krystal and Kisha are both shoeless, walking carefully through the water. Katie and I are lucky to still have our shoes walking over the rocky bottom of the river.

We look up to see how close we are to the bridge and Brad is there! He yells to us, "Hey guys!" Waiving to us as we waive back. There is another man standing with him and he is in his underwear! Can you believe it? Half-Naked Guy is there with Brad! We all walk through the water, dragging our floats behind us, feels like they weigh a ton as we get closer to the bridge. Brad and Half-Naked Guy are smiling. They made a little fire. What's with men and fire? Guess this relationship goes back thousands of years, but I am glad they made one.

Pulling the floats up to the shore, we walk straight to the fire to warm up. I am so ready to go home, but need to dry off a little. We are all soaked to the bone. Half-Naked Guy asks me "Do you want to keep going down the river with me?" I am in shock that he asked me. It's been a while since a guy asked me to do anything, but I shake my head no. "Oh, come on! Let's keep the adventure going, just a couple hours down the river?" "No, sorry, but no." I thought I was very sure about not getting back into the water again, but he is cute. I must be crazy, what am I thinking? No! Maybe we could hang out on dry land, but I'm done with the water for today, for a very long time.

Brad and Krystal hold each other standing next to the fire. They look so happy together. Even after tracking us down for hours, he looks happy to see her happy. Our group makes a circle around the fire to dry off. We ask the guys how they met. Brad says "When I was out looking for you guys last night, I found two guys walking by the bridge and one waived me down. He asked for a ride to his truck, said he was in a hurry to get somewhere." We knew it was Half-Naked Guy's friend. He was in such a hurry, it's as if he was running away from us or running away from the night or maybe that dang river!

Katie says "I'm starving!" and we all agree. We are hungry. Half-Naked Guy says "Let's all go get some breakfast!" "Yes, yes!" we are all in agreement. Then he says "Breakfast is on me!" Krystal and Kisha suggest "How about that Diner on Conner Street?" Sounds expensive to me, but everyone agreed and then Half-Naked Guy says "But I need some clothes to go in there, that's a sit-down restaurant." Krystal says, "If you don't mind pink, I got a sweat shirt and some pants that will fit you." He laughs and says "Ok!" She pulls them out of the back of the truck and passes them to him. He gets dressed, stretching his legs through the jeans, pulling them up, jumping a few times to get in, before zipping them. He pulls the sweatshirt on and all of us girls laugh. Wearing sparkle butt jeans and a pink sweatshirt, he jumps into his jeep. The rest of us, pile into the truck, following behind him to the diner.

We were very lucky to survive the river and we never wanted to get in that water again. But the truth is, we all met back up at Potter's Bridge later that day for a cookout, late in the afternoon, after we all had a nap. Half-Naked Guy was supposed to meet us and bring back the clothes he borrowed, but didn't make it. Probably found a warm, dry bed. And yes, we all got back in, plus Krystal's husband and her boys. I know, I may have looked silly, but this time I brought an umbrella to shield me from the sun. Kind of felt romantic, resting the handle on my shoulder, spinning it, rolling it between my fingers. We learned our lesson and made it a short float. We got out downtown, by the South Side Cemetery. Silly me, I folded up the umbrella and accidentally dropped it in the river, when I hopped off my float to get out of the water. We tried to find it, but no luck. The river giveth and the river taketh, but mostly the river taketh! I'll never forget that day, we were all smiling and kept smiling. For that moment, we were all very happy. I was still in shock that we actually got back into the water, after the night we had.

Our group was soaked, dripping, squeaking and flopping down the side walk. It was a short walk to Krystal's mom's house from the river, less than a block. We threw our floats in her yard, on the soft grass under the shade of a tall tree. Her mom met us on the back porch, smiling, holding a plate of fancy sandwiches she had made for us. We all sat on the deck to dry off, eating our sandwiches and talking about the day and a little about the night on the river.

Acknowledgments

With God all things are possible. I am so grateful for my family and friends. I am very blessed. Thank you, dear Readers, for reading my book. I hope to have the pleasure of sharing another story with you someday.